All night in the new country

MIRIAM BIRD GREENBERG

Miriam Bird greenberg

*To Tim with so much
appreciation and
gratitude, and in the
spirit of future sailing
trips!*

SIXTEEN RIVERS PRESS

Published by Sixteen Rivers Press

P.O. Box 640663

San Francisco, CA 94164

www.sixteenrivers.org

Library of Congress Catalog Card Number: 2013932213

ISBN: 978-1-939639-03-5

Design: Josef Beery

Cover Art: *Sparks* (2012) by Susan Hall,
oil on linen (30 x 40 in.), susanhallart.com

ART WORKS.
arts.gov

Special thanks to the National Endowment for the Arts
for their support of Sixteen Rivers Press

Contents

Before the World Went to Hell

Before the world went to hell my sweetheart
worked at a diner near the marshes
and before that was a physicist in the desert, but now
we were on the move;
the whole country had uprooted—she recognized an old woman
soaking acorns in the river
as a colleague from her first laboratory job. Southerners
had migrated bodily north
leaving fabric shreds in the mesquite, and the West was on fire.
My sweetheart steamed a pot of wild mustard flowers
by the roadside, rain sizzling on the lid. Her shadow,
my breath, the afternoon
that moved on forever: people theorized the earth's orbit
was off-kilter, time
had stopped moving right, and suddenly
though we'd brushed snow
from our walkways
so recently, the sun began to rise two hours earlier. Smoke
gathered in corners
of the sky,
and the peach trees budded, then blossomed
and bore fruit
in a week, but the fruit was mealy and filled with larvae.
This was back when we had walkways,
our own houses, cars, my sweetheart was a stranger

crisp in her lab coat,
and I had never tracked a deer all day then field dressed it
and dragged it home
across wild grass grown tall over an emptied city.

ELEGY

Early on in the city
on weekends claimed by fog
I came back to your farmstead,
your emptied creek-side
shanty house,
from my laboratory wage work
with pockets full of micropipettes
and stolen white gloves as if to outfit a regiment
of ghost butlers
in an imagined antebellum manor
neither of us, if offered, would inhabit—
but I still saw the manor's cut crystal
glinting in night-frost on the fescue
beneath persimmon trees
where great horned owls left
bones to bleach. These nights
lately—with the fine rain singing
through ragweed, through mulberry
we'd kept for feeding ducks, the silkworm
farm we planned
to someday have—I swim
the wild wheat that shines
like a lake to far back acres. I unstring
my jewelry, tarnishing from its work week
even still—in the city of sooted brick and grimy

air—from my neck
and wrists, spread the legs
of the wooden-runged ladder and hang
it in arcs inside the fig bower's
ribcage or hay rick,
displayed like ceremonial
specimens pinned to felt-lined glass cases
by the fig's knobby twigs. Deprived of ceremony
I find nothing
in my hands but unmoored
symbols: one week I caught june bugs in a jar every night
to feed the ducks,
or once burnt so methodically old letters
from lovers and the First National Bank alike,
as if a prayer summoning spirits
to the occasion could ever come
from cynics' lips. To look down
for the layers of history cat's-cradling
between us, which, unwillingly—
as algae on creek stones
loosed downstream rejoins indistinct matter—
we forget.

When I Was a Child

There was a woman who walked the roads all day;
she would come into the café
holding a handkerchief full of bees
then shake them free. You could see her catching them
painstakingly all morning
in the honeysuckle, her face
scabbed where she'd scratched old stings.
She had a daughter
who'd died of lockjaw
after the hospitals had closed;
she was buried by the graves of the great-aunts
who'd raised her, enough
to make anyone crazy. She called
all children her daughter's name. For a time
she slept in the fallen-in blacksmithing
shed in back of our house.
From inside my dreams
I could hear her some nights
calling out, *Ruth, Ruth.*

UTOPIA

The utopia we'd imagined—
of cottonwood water-tracing

and oak-grove windbreaks
(bounded by wrecked strip malls
edged with barbed wire, helicoptered
all night by tobacco-chewing
militiamen)—
           showed its false front

like dirt-yellowed teeth.
                  Million-
watt moons swooped low-slung
over our hideouts, spotlighting
runaways and the bedrolls

abandoned by vagrants
in the overgrowth,
jungles
we'd hoboed and the dim hooch
where I sleep when the tide

goes out of my life
for a while. Our broken-up fire
pits were littered with bones

of small game like when, as kids
on ponies,
                    we chased thicket-
bound coyotes and rabbits
with our badly bred foxhounds
baying (longhaired where ticks
made their nests
                    in neck wrinkles
and paling belly skin), field dressed
critters with a jackknife
to spit-roast on the creek bank.

                              The quarry
where lately I gather mushrooms
earlobed along shallow shaded pools
is a cliff side. Amid a honky fantasy
of Indian afterlife I check my snares

on obscured outcroppings
where cacti tufts keep others (trap
setters, poachers, snake-
oil salespeople with beaded
hair and souring hopes, half-
imaginary

                        but some part true),
away from my catch. I count
constellations in my aerie

some nights as helicopters loop
down into the blast-emptied pits
beneath me, unseeing the eye-
lights of others in their own perches,
tear-edged, worrying their hem-
fray.

                    What promised
land would these creeks and ravines,
harvested for gravestone, for keystones
and curbstones, ever be?

By now the kudzu-claimed cemeteries'
granite was long scavenged
for shanty stoops or sunk
back into faraway earth, swallowed

by the soil like a lure weight.
                    Subterranean
names carved on the stone
sought (like lures) the bodies that bore them:

ghosts rise, moss-fringed
and plain-faced, from the dirt—

decaying suburbia
fills the emptied underground
they've left—they pace, eagle-eyed
for half-smoked cigarettes, hunting

the fallen-in avenues
of a city they've been gone from
too long to have ever,
in their first lives,
come to know.

I Passed Three Girls
Killing a Goat

I passed three girls killing a goat, shotgun
leaned up against a tree and the entrails
spilling into a coil on the ground. It was hooked
between the tendons of its back legs
to a high branch that gently creaked
like a dry hinge busybody aunties wouldn't oil.
Blood drained into a pail—you could smell it
shifting with the air—and black flies landed
in the shadows of things where the wind
didn't touch. I dreamed I was carrying a sack
filled with animals, and it dragged blood
in the gravel and stained my skirt hem; you could follow
my trail to the county line where old men
sat on the liquor store porch. One crooked his half-arm
for the bottle where the auger had caught his hand.
I dreamed I was in a new country rinsing livers
under a spigot, and the men cracking
black walnuts on a stone named my limbs
like the weather, like none of us knew
the same words. By the tree the girls and the goat
were faltering, one squatted to sharpen
her blackened blade on a strop, and the men
on the county line leaned back on the legs
of their chairs talking about anything—each other,

spring weather, the long-haired boy scalped
by a combine—and one of them swore you only plant
beans with the moon in Capricorn, otherwise
the fields choke up with scrub juniper. One
looked intently at his left palm; his right wrist
uselessly brushed the woven seat of his chair.
When a wind came, the screen door leapt up
on its leather hinges, which never creaked,
and slammed shut. Mud daubers in the muck
by the spigot blew sideways around my ankles,
and inside I could hear the woman
who lived with the liquor store proprietor
cursing as she locked up the vanilla like she knew
how to break the back of a ghost.

There Was an Old Legend

There was an old legend
I remembered, of a horse and rider
that haunted mills and fallen-in factories. A nobleman's son,
or laborer, it didn't matter;
this wasn't the kind of country where the lord
took his tithe before the wedding
anymore. Anyway, a young hero
sits awake all night in a haunted mill
to prove his mettle, but by dawn? Nothing
but the wind calling in the trees.
The hero gathers up his blankets and flask
when a howling comes, there's scarcely time to stumble aside
before a horseman gallops past
inside a roar of wind; in his grasp
is a woman's leg, stockinged, which he hurls at the hero.
The hero comes home wild-eyed,
a sole survivor who has climbed
from bloodied wreckage, there's nothing
left for him, he can't hold a job, waits nights in the parking lot
of the grocery store for a jitney fare. Like a talisman
he cannot rid himself of, fine leather shoe
and silk stocking, the night sky hangs its shadows
lower and lower, they sweep his blank face
like the wings
of enormous dark birds.

FALLEN LIMBS LINED THE ROAD

Fallen limbs lined the road,
the roof was dented in
but the doors still shut
so we drove across town to the abandoned school
to play knock rummy on benches
in the dark. The entire town

was black. Across the tracks
where they hadn't yet run
electricity
this year, people sat on their porches
as if nothing

had only just happened.
Rain's history pocked the ditches.
Something stumbled
into shadows
behind the library. Someone with batteries
for their radio danced

alone in their dirt yard across the street.
Nearer, children
clamored in the windblown leaves, probably catching
snakes. A fallen branch
lay across the jungle gym,

its shadows under moonlight
striped my face. I don't quite recall
but that I won
three games in a row
before the night really set in.

It's Hard to Forget

It's hard to forget what I ate when the waters receded:

certain earths, ashes, limestone, cornstalks. Frayed fabric
picked faintly away as if by mice. June bugs. Mice.
I craved friable china clay

from a vein in the pond's berm—ate that, and took duck eggs
to sell in town, though more and more the ducks bore
pale shell-less eggs encased in translucent membrane;
those I tore open, cooked outdoors in a bone-handled coffee can.
Disaster's stratum

marked the abandoned kitchen's clapboard walls
and slat-backed chairs where flooding
had paused for a moment (as if waiting in an orderly way
water has never once done), then moved on. Hemline ravel
threaded to a fine thorn,

I gathered false mending, stitched gold filigree
beneath the fabric folds of a jacket in case one day
it came to me to leave

suddenly. Already half the county had scattered—reedy gullies
gathered left-behind bedrolls, the debris
of mementos too heavy to carry flecking the fields—but thieves

had emptied every barn of its turning forks
and hay hooks, heavier still. Inside mine,
the sun canted

against an aging ox-drawn plow, daybreak sundial
for wanderers to this place inhabited
by wreckage, the packed-dirt floor
specked with bone. Untouched by turmoil,

a pistol lay dissected on the workbench, its interior coils
unsprung, musculature retained in its minute landscape
even still.

Utopia, Again

Afterward we lived five to a room, cooked
on a little alcohol stove by the rag-wrapped spigot
crazed with winter frost shards; summers

we crawled through the underpinnings, shot at rats.
I took care of a hen we kept penned on the windowsill,
took care not to fall in love
                    with more than one person
at once, drank liquor that wouldn't blind me, and cured
twine-bound tobacco that throat-parched and ember-

spat well enough to do anyone in. We ate omelets
every meal and read each other's futures in the yolks.
Those years while revolutions

half a world away coursed through our thoughts
I sat in the basement glued to a ham radio receiver;
men in the hillsides
                    buried barrels of grain
along the perimeters of their property. Others forged knives
in homemade furnaces using creek mud for flux—one,

over radio static, if I met him at the flea market
by the highway, would show *a pretty-sounding woman
like me*   how to dress a rabbit *the right way*.

SOMEONE SUCH AS THIS

After Sherwood Anderson's "Death in the Woods"

There was an old woman who lived in a tar-papered
shack outside of town—she couldn't have been forty
yet, but walked with bowed shoulders. Three dogs
followed her wherever she went; they weren't hers
exactly, but wild, mottled, tick-eared things
perhaps she once gave a piece of liver to, and they
were bound to her as she had once been bound.
Anyone who lives in the country knows someone
such as this, though no one speaks to her. You see her
walking the roadsides some days, and in her you see
your own mother—or in frightening moments, yourself:
bound by a certain predictability of fate that none
see in their youth, though even as a girl she knew
countless older women who sold a few eggs or asparagus
gathered in the woods to buy a scrap of meat,
some flour. Her own future, she would have told you
(if you had asked) would be different than this.

Knowing

On the path
three peasant girls
approached. Really,
they were just like me
but from a different county:
you could tell
by looking, gaps or gold
teeth and blouses embroidered
with wheelbarrows, scythes, tools
made for making things
new, and they wore necklaces
of guinea hen feathers
speckled like the guileless
faces of dice loosed
on dim floorboards just before
loss. Out here where skiffs
prowled the tributaries,
girls pulled each other's teeth
to see the future, threw them
as dice to read the blood-
ied roots' patterns, a map
of the past they couldn't stomach
not knowing. If you were one
of those whose whole family
had slipped out on you

at gunpoint while you slept
undisturbed in the next room,
what did a tooth matter?
So some had mouths full of dark
holes, kept the scrap
of paper scripted with blood
in a close pocket. Even
to me on the path, one girl
with pliers holstered
at her waist spat
through a gap in her grin.
They didn't say it would be
like this, she said, gesturing
at the path, past
and future, dusk,
empty as a smile.

NIGHT TREMBLED ALL AROUND ME

                              Sign
on the door of my travelers' hotel: "Outside
Is Not So Safe," the darkness slipping
its fingers in around the unlatched
lock. But what you really had to watch for
were pits dug in the ground in empty places.
Stumble and you might find yourself
kissing a pale face covered in grief, or eye
to eye with a drowned animal. Borders
shook, sewn shut like sutures fraying
at the edges of the night. Watch carefully
when the moon is at this angle; people
go out to the woods *(no—are sent)* with shovels.
Fallen fruit sweetening the air, pungent
where saplings will sprout from the stones
in spring; but the pits they are digging
are meant   for a different thing.

REMEMBER

Remember the ruined caravan
we approached at dusk where boys lolling on the lip of a well
idly sent three bursts of bullets

into the air, neither welcome
nor threat? Remember, one told us of another who'd fallen
into that same well,

treading water three days
and calling like a baby bird for its mother. Only
they didn't say it like that. One said,

The water here isn't safe
to drink right now, but come to my house for supper;
we boil tea from melted snow.

LOVE POEM

The look some men have in the early morning, light
slanting through the window. As if they'd been born

in a volcano where the boys metamorphosed
during puberty into birds. There's so much

to surmise about rites of passage, but in the end
even ones who brought back rabbits from nights beyond

the brim and rinsed their bloodied hands
in kitchen mop buckets wished to shrug off their bird

bodies as soon as they could. Their mothers learned
to speak bird—only a little magic was necessary—

you could buy tongues harvested from starlings
in a war-ridden country; a mother must speak to her sons

somehow. There are ways of making violence
into an offering. All women grow into knowing

this, bodies verbs in the noun-filled fields of pumice rock
specked with obsidian and the air wild until dusk, tall grass

rustling with voles and rabbits. Overhead, raptors circle
in the cool air, and what can I do but feel my own skin

set around me as if it were fur? No—I mean
when the fireflies first appear we'll want

to paste their luminescent bodies on our skin
like jewel-lit fish living in deep ocean trenches.

Like the fish will want to devour smaller fish.
Or the wolf, smelling carefully every current

of air; the thief, sharpening a penknife idly
beneath a tree before nightfall, each

regarding the object of his affection
gently. The caress a butcher gives the goat,

the steady, swift blade that follows.

KILLING

How the blade was not sharp enough.
How a duck's neck is supple as a thick piece of rope.
How we squatted close to the damp dirt, nighttime
welling around our ankles. The old men
drunk by the gate had gone to their slanting houses;
no one was on the streets. We had a knife at least,
the kind you plunge into soil for cutting roots, blade
sharpened on both sides, but old, really. How I held her,
wings bound against her struggle, my fingertips touching
on her breastbone. I had killed other animals
before, and once a broken-winged songbird
died of fright in my hands, but it is easy
to forget how something goes boneless
from fear. How the smell of shit rose from her warm body
after. Together we carried her in a burlap sack
through the dark streets, and blood bloomed
on the fabric between us and on the street.
She was a talisman through clusters of men,
only boys but larger, conducting transactions
not quietly, and no one spoke to us or met our eyes.
How, even once we plucked her clean and, safe,
someone set a pot to boil, traces of her smell
clung to our hands like strands of fog.
              How my pulse ran in my fingers
like the heartbeat of another thing.

LONG AGO I HEARD FOOTSTEPS

Long ago I heard footsteps
come to the door, and a man

knocking. We've had an accident

up on the road, can you help?
he pled at the unanswered door,

and kept knocking.

He might have been a thief,
but soon enough a woman's howl

lit up the night, and I put a knife
in my belt. Around dawn

I figured their fortunes
might be worth changing.

After All This

The mountainsides
are empty, the crags
uninhabited.
                    Ash pits
have melted to dirt
beneath the fallen leaves. There are no shots.
No firelight
but yours. No train whistles
                        anymore,
or mail routes, no
riverboats or gasoline for chain saws
or the dirt bikes
that had hummed across the valley.
No pack mules stepping carefully
sideways over the rusted chassis
of dirt bikes. No bullets,
no hunters, no fish
                    flashing
in the river. There is no one to track you
to your shelter, to steal your dog,
if you had one,
                    for food. No one
to learn your name and say it after moon-
rise. The communiqués

of the mountainside are spoor and paw-
print; they pattern the ground
                    just beyond
fire fall. Without fear, the act of flight,
what would you have?

I WANT TO TELL YOU

I want to tell you (I said to the man I'd walked beside
for several days now) how I climbed off a train
at its slanted depot
yellowing with dust blown across the desert,
and an old man waiting on the platform
for no one in particular
tapped his snuffbox into the indentation made by
his thumb's tightened tendons (the sky
behind us was streaked with fire)
and gestured for me to come with him. We went to a house
where a couple opened the door at his knock; he handed them
some bills, pushed me inside. This was farther east,
everyone was drunk
by lunchtime (it had gotten loose of the city),
and the woman led me to a bathroom where men
held bottles in one hand (animals
were moving east and groups of humans too).
They were picking at pieces of raw meat in a bucket
with their other hand, throwing it to a baby seal
(everything was hurrying
through the undergrowth
as if ahead of a fire; to the west smoke
gathered at the horizon).

ALL NIGHT IN THE NEW COUNTRY

I.
I went out to buy some bread. The streets
were filled with gusts of wind like wild dogs
roaming. A man stopped to warn me, Stay away
from the south
of the city, everyone carries a knife
in their boot. That night
I dreamed of holding a blade to the throat
of an old lover (no, an old sweetheart);
I meant to frighten someone else
and it worked. Afterward I stroked my sweetheart's
fine hair but did not apologize. The air
wove in my opened window like snake grass
in shallows, and I woke with my own hair
in knots. This place is making me
not myself, I marveled
sadly, opening a sardine can with its small skate key.
In the marshes five dark birds rose skirring away.

II.
All night in the new country
raccoons cried in the trees. Between my house
and the town, a narrow path
through woods, knives hung from the low branches
of cedars: rusted machetes,
and the long, slender blades used for killing
animals. Moonlight reached its pale hand in
through the branches.
There are many ways to talk about loss;
it is like a body walking next to you in the night, ghost
of the lost one keeping you
company, or only your own grief stumbling
beside you in the darkness.

South into the Country of Lost Things

South into the country of lost things
we passed through quiet
villages. The wind sprang up
overnight, and some mornings
we awoke, dunes
in a desert of dust. A fine sand blew in
from the north, and what of emptied
towns after a year of windstorms:
would the rafters and rooflines
show their spines against
the rising soil
of the deserts that gathered
around them? Those years we became
strangers to ourselves and sought the future
in any sign; if the sands
hadn't overtaken the road
we arrived on by morning,
soon enough the winter rains,
or an army whose trajectory
needed no extant path,
would.

The Arrival

We spoke the same language. No,
we did not speak the same language.
We believed in the same gods. No,
we didn't believe in the same gods.
The lavender fields where we first arrived
were forever symbolic to us, the scent
not somnolent but a promise
of our new future. No, none of that.
The boat we stepped ashore from,
it was burned behind us. Perhaps
they thought our people had only one
and if we couldn't leave, no more
would come. No, it was not our only boat,
but though we hoped others would follow,
none did. The reeds we used to make our first bed
bent easily, and we lay together
in it on a cliff side with paths traced
across the rock face. We snared birds
in nets and roasted them on a spit;
we ate greens picked from sparse rock
outcroppings. We kept a torch aflame
all night for protection. We slept safely.
No, our fishing line disappeared
from its reels, our earrings
from our ears. Finally the blankets

that covered us vanished and we woke
shivering in the inky night. The stars
turned slowly around us, night birds
swept their ugly shadows across
the stony path, and we waited.
No, we did not have to wait.

Belief

CAST: SISTER, *an authoritative woman, is pacing the paving stones and chain-smoking. A* CHILD *is at the top of a ladder with a shotgun, protecting the peach orchard from crows. She is wearing a plain school uniform.* ABRAHAM, *a workman, is on the roof with a hammer, pounding at something or another. Perhaps he is fixing it.*

PROPS: *A ladder, a hammer, a shotgun, a peach orchard, a pouch of tobacco.*

Vignette 1

SISTER (*with reverence*): In the beginning God created the owls and the bees, and he saw the world brought out of darkness.

ABRAHAM: Then he created roads to carry the footsteps of men beyond the curve of the earth.

CHILD: And with their footsteps men shattered stones paving the roads into dust. Then God created the goats. (*Long pause while the child surveys the orchard, her shotgun raised.*) And goats created poison ivy to eat, and the Sahara, unexploded ordnance lining the roadsides, and crows in the orchard.

(Child aims at a crow in a nearby peach tree, fires.) Yo, sis! I bagged another one.

ABRAHAM: Then men created hammers to break the world into ruin and piece it back together again. Next, hemmed in by the paths the roads took through each minefield, men invented death.

SISTER *(again with reverence)*: And God saw the world and knew that it was good.

VIGNETTE 2

SISTER *(rolling another cigarette, lighting it, then taking a long drag before beginning to speak)*: In the beginning, God created the brown bear and the tree of flame, each identical above ground as below.

CHILD: Then he made the honey locust tree and the fire pit, the mirror shrouded in a dark house, and the ceiling blackened with soot, and *(sarcastically)* wrote his name in the corner like graffiti gouged in a school desk.

ABRAHAM: Widows took from the locust its thorn as needle and its twisted fibers as thread, and they used these things to mend clothes torn in mourning or by the claws of an animal.

CHILD: Then God created the broken sapling, the over-turned cooking pot, the domesticated guinea hens scattered from their pen and squawking in alarm. He created the volcano, then footsteps left by an animal in its rain of ash. Eventually the archeologist, much later. (*She takes aim at another crow.*)

ABRAHAM: From their rent clothes widows sewed shrouds to veil the mirrors, or flew them like flags above the mouths of untended wells sunk back into the earth.

CHILD: Then the volcano created the carrion-eaters and the circular winds upon which they flew.

SISTER: And God saw the world and knew that it was good.

VIGNETTE 3

SISTER: In the beginning God created the flicker of each match as it is struck, each pupa in its chrysalis, pollen and potsherds, the bones of animals lacing the long, ash-covered roads to the sea—

CHILD (*interjecting with eye-rolling, would-you-believe*): Then God created the burial rite and the cairn of stones, the seventeen-year cicada—

SISTER: And the Southern Hemisphere that lay beyond the sea.

ABRAHAM: It was humans who created the ID card, forged steel, and fingerprints. Pigment, then ink.

CHILD: And where they didn't discover forged steel, bamboo worked just as well. (*Knowingly*) The shape of progress was maintained though its materials varied.

ABRAHAM: And humans wove cages from each new material they discovered, and struck out through the wild tangle of the world into thickets darkness had not yet lifted from, and they brought back two of each creature they encountered, and kept them in cages.

CHILD: And in each cage they placed another human, or an animal, or a cricket and a piece of lettuce, and paraded it through the ash-covered roads, or kept it in a well-guarded cavern, and let it see only enough light to know that light still remained.

ABRAHAM: The captives in their caverns built small cities in the murk, tiny towers looming over the moss-floored marshes.

CHILD: It was *hella dirty;* I seen those cages a couple times before, when I was *younger.*

ABRAHAM: And they carved miniature shackles for each mouse and beetle they saw, and in hunger each fed on each.

CHILD: And the captives made prayers for each new moment that passed, so they might mark it, and make it holy. It was in this way, long ago, that humans created God.

SISTER: And they saw the world, and knew that it was good.

THE END

BORROWINGS

"Night trembled all around her," "She went out to buy some bread," and "In the marshes five dark birds rose skirring away" are taken from Anne Carson's *Men in the Off Hours*.

The story of "I Want to Tell You" belongs to my brother, Alex Bird-Greenberg, and took place in 2004, in Listvyanka, Russia.

ACKNOWLEDGMENTS

Grateful acknowledgment is made to the following journals in which some of these poems first appeared: *Greensboro Review, Killing the Buddha, Nashville Review, Nthposition, Poetry, Salt Hill, Smartish Pace, Stirring, Sycamore Review,* and the anthology *Gulf Stream: Poems of the Gulf Coast.*

Thanks to the Headlands Center for the Arts (where the first poems of this project began while raccoons rattled in the branches outside my window all night), to Sara Peters and Ryan Teitman, and to the careful eye and generous reading of Sixteen Rivers Press and Camille Dungy, who selected this manuscript in the first place. Always to my parents, Evelyn Bird Greenberg and Lester Greenberg; and to Greg Koehler, Peter Mark, Barbara Orlovsky, and David Wevill. But my greatest debt is to the north fork of the Rowdy Creek, overgrown with Osage oranges.

About the Author

Miriam Bird Greenberg grew up on a farm in rural Texas and spent her childhood attempting to communicate with the ghosts who populated her family's century-old homestead. She's held fellowships from the Poetry Foundation, Stanford University, the Provincetown Fine Arts Work Center, and the National Endowment for the Arts (where she is a *2013* Literature Fellow). Greenberg lives in Berkeley, where she teaches English as a Second Language, though in the past she's ridden freight trains across the United States and taught elsewhere in this country, as well as in Canada, and Japan.

Sixteen Rivers Press is a shared-work, nonprofit poetry collective
dedicated to providing an alternative publishing avenue for
San Francisco Bay Area poets. Founded in 1999 by seven writers,
the press is named for the sixteen rivers that flow into San Francisco Bay.

SAN JOAQUIN • FRESNO • CHOWCHILLA • MERCED • TUOLUMNE
STANISLAUS • CALAVERAS • BEAR • MOKELUMNE • COSUMNES
AMERICAN • YUBA • FEATHER • SACRAMENTO • NAPA • PETALUMA